Published by Sweet Cherry Publishing Limited
Unit 36, Vulcan House,
Vulcan Road,
Leicester, LE5 3EF
United Kingdom

First published in the US in 2022
2022 edition

2 4 6 8 10 9 7 5 3 1

ISBN: 978-1-78226-503-0

© Harry Meredith

Soccer Rising Stars: Kylian Mbappé

Cover design and illustrations
by Sophie Jones

Lexile® code numerical measure L = Lexile® 970L

www.sweetcherrypublishing.com

Printed and bound in Turkey

SOCCER RISING STARS

KYLIAN MBAPPÉ

THE UNOFFICIAL STORY

Written by

HARRY MEREDITH

Sweet Cherry

CONTENTS

1
PASSING
THE BATON

Excitement brewed at Ak Bars Arena in Kazan, Russia. 45,000 determined fans had got their hands on tickets to watch a 16-16 tie in the 2018 World Cup. On one side were the feisty and talented Argentinians, led by captain Lionel Messi—one of the greatest

soccer players of the twenty-first century. Messi headed into battle alongside highly-rated players such as Ángel Di María, Sergio Agüero and Javier Mascherano. On the other side was a talented French team, led by their captain Hugo Lloris. Lloris took to the field with teammates Paul Pogba, Antoine Griezmann, N'Golo Kanté and Olivier Giroud.

Although Argentina were heading into the match with a soccer legend, France had the player everyone wanted to see: Kylian Mbappé—a young forward with lightning fast

speed, and tipped by some to be a once-in-a-generation-superstar. This day wasn't just about France vs Argentina, or even 11 vs 11. It was about old vs new. Who would prevail? Messi or Mbappé?

France struck first. During an Argentinean attack, the ball fell loose in France's half. With most of the opposition out of position, Kylian pounced on the loose ball as he saw the perfect opportunity to counterattack. With his blistering pace, he took the ball under his

control and sprinted forward. Three defenders chased behind him, but they had no chance of catching up. In the space of a few seconds, Kylian had left his own half behind and made it to the edge of the penalty box. But as he tried to squirm past the last line of defense, Kylian was dragged to the ground by Marcos Rojo.

"Foul, ref!" Kylian raised his arms in the air in protest, as did his teammates. The referee, without hesitation, pointed to the spot. It was a penalty to France.

Griezmann picked up the ball. He placed it delicately on the penalty spot and stepped backward. He stood with his hands on his hips, visualizing where the ball would hit the net. The Argentinian goalkeeper, Franco Armani, stood tall with his arms pointed out like a starfish, trying to make the target look as small as possible to Griezmann.

The referee blew his whistle. As Griezmann ran to the ball and hit it, Armani dived to his right. But the second the ball left Griezmann's boot, Armani knew he'd made the wrong choice. The ball struck the middle of the net firmly. *Goal!* Griezmann celebrated with Kylian and the rest of the French team. There were thirteen minutes on the clock and it was 1-0. They had the lead.

Argentina fought back in the 41st minute. Èver Banega played a neat pass to Di María outside of the box. He was too far out to score, surely? The talented winger didn't think so! He pulled his left foot back and released a rocket of a shot.

All the French defenders could do was watch the

ball blast past them toward the goal. The French goalkeeper, Lloris, dived toward it. But the ball had been hit with such force and accuracy that it flew past Lloris and into the net. The Argentinian fans were sent into a cheering frenzy. Di María ran toward the fans with his arms wide, shouting at the top of his lungs.

At halftime the teams headed into the dressing rooms. Both sides had struck the net, but at the halfway point it was still all to play for.

Argentina came out fighting in the second half and they earned a free

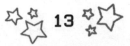

kick to the side of the box in the 48th minute. Banega dinked the ball into the box, but it was headed away by a French defender. The ball fell to the player on the field capable of turning any opportunity into a goal. Off balance, Lionel Messi took the ball under his control and turned. He curled the ball toward the goal. Still standing in the box as a result of the free kick, Gabriel Mercado was free. Messi's effort was heading toward the defender, so Mercado nimbly flicked the ball into the net, giving Lloris no chance. *Goal!* Argentina

may have let in the first, but they had now scored two goals and were in the lead.

Kicked into gear after falling behind, France began their fightback. In the 57th minute, Lucas Hernández sprinted down the left flank before firing in a cross. It flew in behind his team's attackers, and the chance seemed to have gone. However, running toward the opposite corner of the box was French right back Benjamin Pavard. He let off a shot like a prayer to the skies, going against the spin of the ball and

sending it swerving into the net.
Goal! Once again the teams were
level, and France had just scored one
of the best goals of the tournament.

As the players walked back into
position, Kylian was called over
by the French manager, Didier
Deschamps.

"It's your turn now. This is the
stage where legends are made," said
Deschamps. "Show them what you
can do!"

In the 64th minute, Hernandez
sent in a cross from the left. Kylian
controlled the ball in a crowded box

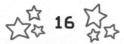

and wriggled his way through the defense. With his weaker left foot, he struck at the goal and the ball squirmed underneath the goalkeeper. Kylian slid on his knees in front of the crowd and performed his

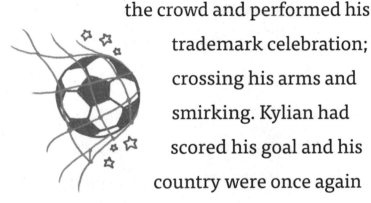

trademark celebration; crossing his arms and smirking. Kylian had scored his goal and his country were once again in the lead, 3-2.

However, the young Frenchman was far from finished. Only four minutes later, Kylian and France

were on the counterattack. Giroud gracefully played a through ball to the onrushing Kylian. No one could catch him. With his right foot he hit the ball into the net with venom. *Goal!* The French substitutes joined in with the celebrations as Kylian announced himself on the biggest soccer stage. Argentina were able to grab a goal back in stoppage time, with a Sergio Agüero header, but Kylian had already placed the final nail in the coffin. The final whistle blew. France and Kylian were on their way to a World Cup quarterfinal.

The great Lionel Messi stood in the center of the field staring sadly into the crowd. Understanding the heartbreak of the opposition, Kylian walked over to the defeated Argentine.

"Hold your head high," said Kylian. "You played a great game."

"Thanks," said Messi. "I'm going to need to keep an eye on you."

"Why's that?" asked Kylian.

"Because you're going to do great things. I know it."

France had beaten Argentina and new had triumphed over old. Now

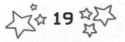

France were on target to achieve
something even more incredible:
they had every shot at winning the
World Cup. They had one of the most
talented and promising rising stars
of the soccer world. It was beginning
to look like they could achieve
anything with Kylian Mbappé on
their team.

2

RAISED
BY BONDY

Kylian was born on the 20th of
December 1998, in the suburb of Bondy
in Paris. Bondy was known by some
for being violent and dangerous. It
was not an area that anyone expected
one of the world's most exciting soccer
talents to come from.

Kylian's mother, Fayza Lamari, was a talented handball player. While his father, Wilfried Mbappé, was a coach for the local soccer club. Many parents like to say that their child was born with a ball by their feet. But with Kylian Mbappé, this saying could very well have been true.

AS Bondy, the club his father coached at, was a well-run team that played in the lower tiers of the French soccer pyramid. It meant that Kylian grew up in an environment of youth soccer and with a passion for the sport in his blood.

"Happy birthday, son!" said Kylian's father one day, opening the door to their kitchen.

Three-year-old Kylian, only just tall enough to reach the kitchen counter, turned to his father with a smile. Placed on the counter was a present almost as big as he was. Kylian's eyes widened and he couldn't stop himself from jumping up and down with excitement. He'd never had a present that big before.

"Can I open it, can I open it, can I open it? Pleeeeease?" said Kylian.

Kylian's father picked up the

wrapped present and placed it on the floor. As Kylian went toward it, his mother put her arm in front of him.

"What do we say?" she said.

"Thank you," said Kylian.

His mother released him and he ripped through the wrapping paper like a lion devouring its dinner. It was a 4x4 toy car, large enough for Kylian to sit in. Delighted, he jumped into it and started moving the steering wheel.

"Vroom vroooooom!" he said, with an intensity that made his parents cry with laughter.

Kylian loved his new toy. While he grew up in a suburb where money was often hard to come by, his parents always tried their hardest to provide him with the best care and love. One of the first questions he asked after getting his toy car was whether he could ride it to the soccer field across the street. Although he loved his new toy car very much, something else had already stolen his heart. Ever since Kylian could walk, he only had eyes for soccer. When Kylian wasn't playing on the street opposite his house, he was watching people play

at AS Bondy while his father coached. The moment he was old enough, Kylian started to make his way through the club's youth setup. It was always obvious that he had a talent to be admired.

Kylian played in matches at AS Bondy and outside of the club, too. One of the most important annual tournaments was played at his school. Mixed year and gender groups played against one another for a cheap plastic trophy and bragging rights. While the prize was nothing but a piece of plastic,

winning it meant the world to young kids in the sixth to ninth grade. Kylian wanted to win the cup so badly one year that he told a friend he'd buy them a coloring book if they gave 100% effort on the field. He even received nine warnings from his teachers in a single day, because whether he was in mathematics, history or science class, he talked about nothing but soccer.

Despite these warnings Kylian's soccer dreams never faded. With a close family and a supportive community, Kylian was given the

platform to thrive. He had everything he needed from those close to him, even in a suburb that—from the outside looking in—seemed like one where dreams went unrealized. Kylian promised himself that he would represent his community and bring them success.

He was Kylian Mbappé, the son of two caring parents, a product of his suburb, AS Bondy and the community that had helped raise him. He was going to do everything he could to make them proud.

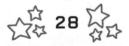

3
AN ENGLISH ADVENTURE

"Enjoy your flight," said the flight attendant, as 11-year-old Kylian rushed up the boarding stairs onto the plane. He worked his way through the aisle before finding his seat. Not far behind him were his father and mother.

"I get the window!" said Kylian,

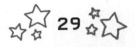

darting to his seat and plunging into the pouch of magazines in front of him. "How long will the flight be again?"

"About the same time as a soccer match ..." his father grinned.

After a few minutes of staring out of the window, the seatbelt sign above Kylian turned on.

"If you could please fasten your seatbelts. Your flight from Paris to London will be leaving shortly," said the attendant through the loudspeaker

Kylian and his family did not often leave Paris, let alone France, but there

was an important reason for their departure. Kylian had been talent-spotted by a Chelsea scout while playing in a match. He had been invited for a week's trial at Cobham training ground for the Chelsea FC Academy. Kylian was nervous. He'd never done anything like this before, but his nerves were also joined by an endless excitement and adrenaline rush. He was used to playing soccer at the park, or at best playing in small stadiums. Never before had he trained at a professional setup as glamorous and modern as Chelsea's.

When the family arrived, they took in as many sights as they possibly could before training started. They were almost as excited to see London as they were for Kylian to train with Chelsea. They visited Buckingham Palace, admired Big Ben and went for a stroll in Hyde Park.

At Cobham, Kylian was given a tour of the facilities. His eyes lit up as he was shown the many fields, dressing rooms and state-of-the-art facilities that had only recently been upgraded. He'd never seen a training facility this impressive before.

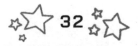

Kylian trained with the Chelsea FC academy for a few days and took part in a game against fellow London side Charlton Athletic. Chelsea was victorious with an 8-0 thrashing, showing that this was an academy overflowing with talent. Kylian impressed the coaches, and as a reward for his hard work he was invited to meet the Chelsea manager at the time, Carlo Ancelotti. But this meeting was not the only one that the club had arranged.

"Could you come with me?" said one of the Chelsea coaches.

Kylian followed the coach away from the training field and into the facility. Standing inside, looking at a poster on the wall, was none other than Didier Drogba. Chelsea's legendary striker, known for his strength, ferocity and incredible goalscoring skills, turned and smiled at the young Kylian.

"Hello," said Drogba. "You must be Kylian."

Kylian froze by the door. He was meeting a real professional soccer player. One he'd seen on TV

hundreds of times, and he was now standing right in front of him.

"Hi," said Kylian. "You're so good!"

Drogba laughed. "I've heard you're good too."

Chelsea presented Kylian with his own shirt, with the number 10 on the back, and offered him a place in the academy. Yet to Chelsea's surprise, and Kylian's disappointment, the offer was rejected.

"Why do I have to say no?!" asked Kylian, in the car on the way home from training.

"You know why," said his mother.

"It's better for you to learn in France."

"But it's fun here," said Kylian.

"There are many teams interested in you," said his father. "This is the first offer, but it won't be the last."

The Mbappés had always planned for a future in France. They feared that in a faraway country, under the guidance of a soccer superpower, it would be all too easy for Kylian to be swept up in a production line of soccer players. Therefore, they had always known that Kylian's future was in Paris. Despite Chelsea's best efforts, Kylian turned down the offer

and returned home with his family.
The next task was convincing his
schoolmates on the playground that
he had met Didier Drogba.

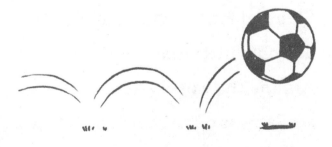

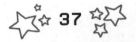

CLAIREFONTAINE ACADEMY

In the north of France, not too far away from Paris, lies the heart of French soccer. It is known as INF Clairefontaine, or Institut National du Football de Clairefontaine. Around the world this soccer academy is often said to be the best.

It's the place for young soccer players to hone both their technical and tactical abilities, making sure they become the "perfect player". Not only is it the home of elite youth soccer training, but it is also the base of the French national team. Every year the academy runs trials to scout the most promising local soccer talents from the Paris suburbs. A handful of players between the ages of 12-15 are given the chance to impress and potentially set themselves on a path to soccer stardom.

Not too long after returning from England, Kylian took part in Clairefontaine trials. He excelled during every showing and was selected as one of the new intakes for the academy. He trained with them on Sundays through to Fridays before returning to AS Bondy on Saturdays to take part in their fixtures. To some, playing soccer every single day of the week would be too much. But to Kylian it was perfect. He got to do what he loved every single day of the week, and he wouldn't have traded it for anything.

However, Kylian's first year at the academy wasn't always easy. For being one of the youngest in the group he was known as the baby, earning the nickname 'Mbebe'. Every morning he would have classes, followed by an afternoon filled with soccer exercises—a mixture of ball work, athletic training and positional awareness. There was no time for distractions. There wasn't even the possibility of them, as the players were only allowed to use their mobile phones for a short time at the end of the day.

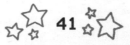

Kylian's concentration was purely focused on classes and soccer.

At Clairefontaine the focus was on the individual player rather than on the team. The aim was to make each player the best in their position and, as a result, create a group of superior players. One of the primary goals during the first year is for players to work on their weaker foot. But when Kylian returned to play for AS Bondy on Saturdays, his father wasn't too happy with this experimental approach.

Kylian was on the right wing for AS Bondy. He was playing in a league match for the team and his father was barking orders to the players on the touchline. The ball made its way to Kylian and instead of using his dominant foot to pass to the player near him, he used his weaker foot and attempted to play a cross-field pass to his teammate. The pass was close, but not close enough, and was stolen by the opposition.

While this form of trial and error was needed to develop a complete soccer player, at AS Bondy the

focus was on results rather than an individual's development.

Kylian soon learned to play in a more controlled way when returning to AS Bondy. But as he battled his way through a tough first year, the fruits of his efforts began to show. He was far more effective with his weaker foot and was developing into an exceptional athlete.

This development continued during his second year at Clairefontaine and was noticed by the professional clubs monitoring his progress.

On the week of Kylian's 14th birthday, he received an invitation to another trial. As a reward for Kylian's hard work, his family agreed that he could go. This time his trial was not in England, but in Spain. Kylian had been invited to train with none other than the 'Galácticos'. He was going to play soccer at Real Madrid.

Kylian traveled to the Spanish capital with his family, in the same way that they had gone to London during his trial at Chelsea. But, as with the trip to London, Kylian's parents saw the trial as a gift for their son.

They never intended to accept an offer for him to join the academy.

Kylian's soccer idol was Cristiano Ronaldo: arguably the greatest soccer player of the modern era. In his childhood bedroom in Bondy, Kylian had posters of Ronaldo covering his bedroom walls. He often went to sleep dreaming of being as good as the famous number 7, and on this trip he was potentially going to meet his idol. Kylian could hardly contain his excitement. During his first training session at Real Madrid, he was greeted by none other than

Zinedine Zidane. Then, after lining up with the other prospects, Kylian got what he wanted most.

A picture with Cristiano Ronaldo!

When he met his idol, Kylian was unable to resist performing Ronaldo's iconic celebration. Kylian jumped in the air and pointed to the back of his shirt yelling, "SIIIIIIII!"

Ronaldo laughed. "I like your celebration. Let's have a photo."

Ronaldo put his arm around Kylian and they both smiled as a photographer took the picture.

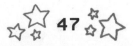

"You're my favorite player!" said Kylian.

"I'm honored," Ronaldo smiled. "I'm sure *you'll* be someone's favourite player in the future."

Like their English adventure, Kylian and his family returned from the experience in Spain feeling inspired. Yet they never considered changing Kylian's path. The young star was to continue his soccer education in France.

However, his time at Clairefontaine was approaching its end. And there was so much interest in Kylian that

it seemed he had more suitors than there were teams in the league! The question on everyone's mind was: what team would Kylian choose?

5
MOVING TO
MONACO

Out of the tens, if not hundreds of club offers on the table, Kylian opted for the historic AS Monaco. They were a top side, competing in the French premier league—Ligue 1— and were known for their effective and competitive academy setup.

What made Kylian choose Monaco was the reassurance that he would be provided with a path to the first team when the time was right. Many young talents before him had spent years on the bench, or had to move out on loan to lower division sides to play first team soccer. But Kylian moved to Monaco and excelled in their academy. When the time was right, just as the coaches had promised, he was given the chance to play in his first professional match.

On the 2nd of December 2015, Kylian made a brief appearance in a

league match against Stade Malherbe Caen. The match finished as a 1-1 draw, and Kylian played for only a handful of minutes. It was not a memorable debut for the spectators, or for the press, but to Kylian it meant everything. He became AS Monaco's youngest ever debutant at the age of 16 years and 347 days. It was a record that, up until that point, had been held by none other than fellow Clairefontaine graduate and French soccer legend, Thierry Henry.

Although Kylian had not excited or dazzled during his debut, his hard

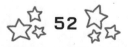

work in training and obvious talents earned him lots of chances to play for the first team. The majority of these opportunities were brief substitute appearances.

A few months after his debut, Kylian scored his first ever goal for AS Monaco. During a seventeen-minute appearance he scored in a 3-1 win against fellow league side Troyes. And as he did so, another record fell. Kylian became the club's youngest

 ever goalscorer. It was to be his only league goal during the 2015/2016 campaign.

Kylian returned for his second season at AS Monaco a changed player. During his debut season, Paris Saint-Germain had won the league with ease. Everyone in soccer expected them to do the same in the 2016/2017 Ligue 1. But with a team filled with talent, a leading manager and an emerging superstar in Kylian Mbappé, AS Monaco were about to disrupt any sense of normality within French soccer.

With two games left to play, all AS Monaco needed was a single point to claim the Ligue 1 title in a home tie against AS Saint-Étienne. Up front AS Monaco had the experienced striker Radamel Falcao and tricky wingers in the form of Bernardo Silva and Thomas Lemar. It was a frightening forward line. In defense they had two menacing fullbacks in Benjamin Mendy and Djibril Sidibé, not to mention the towering Kamil Glik in central defense and shot stopper Danijel Subašić in goal.

The finest jewel in their crown was Kylian Mbappé. With his lightning pace and incredible goalscoring prowess, the young Frenchman was

an unstoppable force in the league.

In the 19th minute of the match, with the home fans roaring, Kylian ran onto a through ball and made his way into the opposition's box. The goalkeeper raced out to close him down, so Kylian feinted to shoot with his right and tricked the keeper. Instead, he moved to the left and tapped the ball into an empty net. Kylian and AS Monaco held on to the lead, even adding to it with a stoppage time goal from Valére Germain. As the final whistle

blew it was official—PSG had been dethroned. Kylian and AS Monaco were Ligue 1 champions!

Yet the team's success did not only come in the form of a league triumph. Kylian and AS Monaco emerged from a Champions League group containing Tottenham Hotspur, Bayer 04 Leverkusen and CSKA Moscow. In the following round of 16, they faced Pep Guardiola's Manchester City.

Kylian and AS Monaco shocked the world by knocking Manchester City out of the competition on away goals

with a 6-6 scoreline on aggregate.
The team then went on to defeat
Borussia Dortmund over two legs in
the quarterfinals, too, before finally
falling to the Italian side Juventus.
During this run Kylian scored six
Champions League goals.

Before the season, not many
had seen AS Monaco as a major
European soccer power. But to every
soccer fan in the world there was
now no question. The French team
had put together a team of stars and
the brightest of them all was Kylian
Mbappé.

As the season came to a close, every major soccer team in France started to open their wallets and put together plans on how to attract this talent. Every manager was desperate to buy Kylian Mbappé.

6

BLUE, WHITE AND RED

It wasn't only clubs that had taken notice of Kylian's unrivaled rise to the top. The coach of the national team was paying attention too. Didier Deschamps, the manager of France, included Kylian in his squad for a World Cup Qualifying match

and friendly. The 18-year-old had been tearing up both Ligue 1 and the Champions League. Although he was young, the manager didn't hesitate to call up the talented forward.

While Kylian was able to briefly return to the academy at Clairefontaine with the national team, he did not get to stay there for long. The qualifier was taking place on foreign shores and in a rather peculiar location. France were playing away in Luxembourg. Instead of in a famous stadium teeming with fans, Kylian would be making his

international debut in one of Europe's smallest countries. However, this in no way took the shine off of Kylian's call-up. Only a few years ago, he had been kicking a ball about with his friends in a park pretending to be his national team heroes. But now, he wasn't going to be pretending. He would be the player children across France dreamt of being.

France's team bus arrived at Stade Josy Barthel, a stadium in Luxembourg's capital. With a maximum capacity of 8,125 fans, it certainly wasn't Kylian's largest audience. France, sitting comfortably at the top of their qualifying group, were expected to win the match with ease. Despite their underdog status, the home fans were intent on wildly cheering for their team in this qualifying match. With a ton of talent within the squad, Kylian had been named on the substitutes bench.

As expected, France took the lead via an Olivier Giroud strike. But the underdogs took everyone by surprise by responding with a goal of their own only six minutes later. Luxembourg's Aurélien Joachim

scored from the penalty spot to the delight of the home crowd. The equalizer brought about an enormous cheer from the home support, yet their smiles did not last for long. France regained the lead within three minutes via a penalty conversion of their own from Antoine Griezmann. The French team went into the locker room at the end of the first half with a slim lead, against a side that they should, on paper, have been beating comfortably. The French manager was far from pleased.

"You need to do better," said Deschamps, pacing around. "You're playing at 50%. They shouldn't have a chance to grab your shirts let alone score against you!"

The coach picked up a bottle of water and finished it, giving himself a moment to calm down. He screwed on the lid, and softly placed it into a bin.

"We're winning and that's good," he continued. "But you know you can do more."

The players prepared themselves for the second half. One by one they

exited the locker room and headed to the field.

"Mbappé," said the coach.

Kylian stayed back as the rest of the players left.

"I'll make no promises, but if the team plays better in the second half, you'll get some game time."

Kylian nodded. On the outside he wanted to present a professional and calm manner. But inside he felt like  a firework about to go off. Kylian held himself back from letting his excitement show.

As the second half began, at first
it seemed that the coach's team talk
had not spurred on the team, as it was
Luxembourg who came out fighting.
However, Giroud grabbed his second
goal of the night in the 76th minute.
He eased the manager's worries and
put his country into a 1-3 lead.

As promised, Kylian was asked
to warm up. In the 78th minute, he
became not just a professional soccer
player, but a national team player
too. Kylian high-fived the departing
Dimitri Payet and sprinted onto the
field.

His brief appearance at the end of the match was filled with darting runs, neat passes and measured play. The game came to an end with the score still at 1-3. France took home the three points and Kylian was given his first ever national team appearance. As the final whistle blew, no player had a bigger grin on their face than Kylian Mbappé.

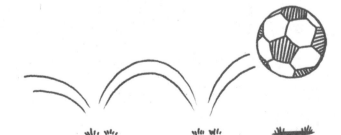

7
COMING HOME

While Kylian had completed his first season in French soccer as a relative unknown on the world stage, that was far from the case with his second season. After his unforgettable campaign, it was clear to the world that Kylian Mbappé

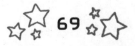

was an incredible talent. A talent so impressive that if a club wanted to acquire him, they would have to part with an enormous fee—perhaps even a record-breaking one.

There were only a handful of clubs that had the spending power to buy Kylian. Real Madrid, just as they had tried to sign him for their academy, once again tried to lure him to Spain. But to the surprise of many, it was a club much closer to home that Kylian moved to.

In the past, if a player of Kylian's talent was on the transfer market they would often leave for the riches and success found in the Premier League or La Liga. Yet this French talent decided that it wasn't time for him to leave his country. It was time for him to return home and sign for Paris Saint-Germain, with the aim of not only raising his superstar status, but of making a club in France one of the best in the world.

Kylian joined PSG on a one-year loan with the option to buy for €180 million. This made his transfer the second largest in soccer history at the time, following PSG's €222 million

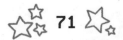

purchase of Neymar in the same summer. Kylian was returning to the city that made him—to the team that many of his friends and family had supported growing up. Now he'd be the one on the famous Parc des Princes field aiming to bring soccer glory to the French capital.

It didn't take long for Kylian to settle into his new team. He'd spent

the majority of his life in Paris, so getting used to the surroundings was never going to be an issue. Kylian scored thirteen goals and provided seven assists during his first Ligue 1 campaign with PSG. He played his part not only in winning the league trophy for his side that year, but also in a domestic treble. PSG were the season's champions of Ligue 1, and winners of the Coupe de France and Coupe de la Ligue.

After his trophy haul there was no time for Kylian to rest in the summer of 2018. He was selected by Didier Deschamps to be a member of France's 2018 World Cup squad. Could Kylian repeat his club success in the national team? Could he end

the summer with not only league and domestic cup medals around his neck, but a World Cup winner's medal too?

8
WORLD CUP 2018

The moment Kylian and the French team set foot on Russian ground there was a feeling of optimism. A feeling that, with this talented crop of players, they had a real opportunity at winning. But talented teams had failed in the past, and at

this famous tournament they were certainly not the only team filled with world-class players. However, they were the only team with Kylian Mbappé.

France passed through the group stages comfortably, beating Australia and Peru in their opening two matches before drawing with a stubborn Danish side. Kylian then played a crucial role in the 16-16 tie against Argentina, providing two goals and one assist. France came out on top, in one of the standout matches of the tournament.

France then made their way past another fierce South American side —Uruguay—in their quarterfinal to set up a semifinal against Belgium. Both France and Belgium played well, but a header from a corner by French defender Samuel Umtiti was the difference maker in a 1-0 victory. Kylian and his teammates had played themselves into a World Cup final! The last team standing in their way was Croatia—a side that many had not picked to make it to the final. But with their brilliant midfielder and

captain, Luka Modrić, they had beaten every team that had crossed their path. They weren't pushovers, and Kylian and France had to perform at their best if they wanted to win.

Thirty-two teams had become two. The final was taking place in Russia's capital city of Moscow. Packed into Luzhniki Stadium were 81,000 fans sitting, standing and shouting in preparation for a nail-biting match. In their instantly recognizable red and white checkered uniform, the Croatian fans were rowdy and excited. The same could be said about the

French fans, cheering as a mass of blue, white and red.

Kylian and his teammates walked out of the tunnel as did their opposition. Placed on a stand in front of them was the World Cup trophy. Every player gazed at the trophy as they walked past it. They were only ninety minutes away from glory. Only one soccer match away from writing their names into the history of soccer.

In the 18th minute, France earned a free kick in Croatia's half. It was too far out to shoot, so the left-footed

Griezmann opted to dink the ball into the box in the hope that a teammate could get their head to it. He crossed the ball and it headed toward goal. In desperation, as an attempt to defend the cross, Croatian striker Mario Mandžukić tried to head it away. But instead, the ball grazed the top of his head and chipped over his goalkeeper. *Goal!* Kylian celebrated with his teammates as the French fans roared with cheers.

This setback motivated the Croatian side. Ten minutes later they earned a free kick. Modrić

chipped the ball to the right side of the box where it was kept alive by Šime Vrsaljko. After bouncing around in the box, Croatia's Domagoj Vida took the ball under his control and set it back to the edge of the box. Ivan Perišić created space by knocking the ball to his left and released a thunderous strike at goal. It powered through the mass of bodies in the box and the goalkeeper flung himself at it. But the ball was traveling too fast and

it smashed into the back of the net. *Goal!* The game was level.

Perišić was the hero, but minutes later he quickly became the villain. From a corner, the ball struck his hand and the VAR deemed it a handball. France had won a penalty! Griezmann took on the responsibility, firing his penalty coolly to the left of the goal while the goalkeeper dived to his right. *Goal!* France were back in the lead.

In the second half Paul Pogba played a volley that cut through Croatia's defense. The lightning

quick Kylian was the first to the ball and brought it under his control. Whenever Kylian was on the ball the Croatian defense was terrified, not knowing how to deal with his unstoppable pace. Kylian performed step overs on the corner of the box before driving toward the byline. His cross was defended, but bounced kindly to Griezmann, who set the ball back to Pogba. Pogba shot with his right foot, but the ball was blocked valiantly by a Croatian defender. However, the ball bounced straight back to Pogba and he was gifted

a second chance. This time he wouldn't miss. With his left foot he carefully guided the ball toward goal. The unbalanced keeper, Subašić, could do nothing as the net behind him rippled. *Goal!* Even for a top side like Croatia, it was a tough ask for them to recover.

The French fans in the stadium went wild! They were only half an hour away from World Cup glory. Little did they know that only five minutes later, their smiles would be even wider.

Theo Hernández made his way

down the left flank, twisting and turning between defenders before finding Kylian free in the center. Kylian took one touch to receive the ball, another to push it to the right and a third to shoot. From outside of the box, the ball fired across the ground and into the corner of the net. *Goal!* Kylian ran to the corner with his arms outstretched. The

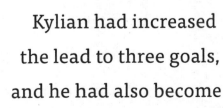

substitutes ran onto the field to celebrate with him.

Kylian had increased the lead to three goals, and he had also become

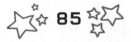

only the second teenager to score
in a World Cup final after the
legendary Brazilian striker Pelé.
This was Kylian's crowning moment.
He was the boy with the world at
his feet.

Croatia were able to score one
more goal thanks to a lapse in
concentration by the French
goalkeeper, Hugo Lloris. Softening
the blow of having scored an own

goal earlier in the match,
Mandžukić pounced on a
loose touch by Lloris and
passed it into the net. But

in the remaining minutes of the match, France kept their cool. The substitutes lined up by the technical area with their bibs removed. Every squad member was ready to sprint onto the field and release every emotion that they had bottled up through the tournament. The referee blew the whistle. It was official: Kylian Mbappé and France were world champions! The substitutes sprinted onto the field and the coaches embraced.

"We did it!" Kylian yelled, running to his captain, Pogba.

"Wooooo! Vive la France!" Pogba
yelled as they jumped up and down,
with joy.

9
GIVING BACK

Kylian returned to Paris not as a soccer hero but as an icon. Almost every child across the country was playing soccer in their gardens, nearby fields and parks, trying to recreate his famous performances.

One of Kylian's first acts when he returned home was to give back.

For his involvement in the World Cup winning campaign, Kylian received €400,000. Instead of keeping the money, Kylian donated it to Premiers de Cordeé: a children's charity that helps run sports activities for disabled and hospitalized children. While many soccer players might have been considering what flashy car to buy next, Kylian was playing on AstroTurf with the children. Some said that Kylian had so much fun participating in these games that he enjoyed it more than the kids did!

Fans gathered around the artificial grass to watch as Kylian played.

"Out wide!" said Kylian. A young girl in a wheelchair knocked the ball to Kylian. He took it under his control and softly passed the ball in front of the goal. The young girl met the ball and knocked it into the net. *Goal!*

Kylian celebrated and so did everyone watching. The young girl shot an infectious smile at Kylian and copied his famous celebration by crossing her arms.

But being a patron for a charity wasn't enough for Kylian.

Understanding that his actions could mean the world to young fans, he decided to set up his own charity. With the help of his mother, Kylian set up 'Inspired by KM': a charity created to help children between the ages of 9–14 achieve their dreams, whether that was becoming the Kylian Mbappé of mathematics or embarking on a career in medicine.

Because he had grown up in the poor neighborhood of Bondy, Kylian understood the disadvantages and struggles that the children had to go through. Now that he was

achieving his goals, he saw it as his responsibility to help the community that raised him. His new goal was to give back, and to help hundreds of children just like himself accomplish the unthinkable.

10
PLAYER OF THE YEAR

Kylian brought his unstoppable form from the World Cup back into the new league season. During the 2018/2019 Ligue 1 season, Kylian was every defender's worst nightmare. He was quick, intelligent and deadly in front of goal. Kylian led PSG to yet

another Ligue 1 title. In the process he scored a mind-boggling thirty-three goals and provided nine assists.

As a result of his incredible playing, Kylian was invited to the end-of-year award ceremony known as the Tropheés UNF du football. Here, players and managers from both Ligue 1 and Ligue 2 are recognized for their efforts during the season.

Kylian arrived on the red carpet dressed in a pristine black suit. Cameras flashed as he walked down the carpet and the paparazzi shouted for his attention. In the chaos he made

sure to stop and sign autographs for the children in the crowd. He posed in front of the sponsored boards before making his way to his seat in the beautifully decorated hall. Hundreds of people were scattered across finely decorated tables.

Kylian was awarded as not just a member of the Team of the Year, but as the Young Player of the Year too. However, the biggest prize remained unclaimed. It was time to announce the Player of the Year award. Announcing this year's winner was none other than Didier Drogba—

the striker Kylian had once gazed at in amazement all those years ago at Chelsea.

"And the award goes to ..." said Drogba. "Kylian Mbappé."

The crowd applauded and Kylian went to the stage to collect his third award of the evening.

"I guess they weren't kidding when they said you were good," joked Drogba, handing him the award.

In his speech, Kylian thanked his family, his friends and his teammates, not forgetting all of his fans who had supported him through his career.

 97

Kylian took this winning energy into the following league campaign. Once again, he finished as the league's top scorer with eighteen goals and seven assists, and Paris Saint-Germain claimed the Ligue 1 title. Meaning that with AS Monaco and PSG, Kylian had won the league four years in a row.

Kylian and the club were delighted to win the league. But there was another trophy that they sought more than anything else. A trophy that consistently avoided their grasp. Would they ever win the Champions League?

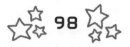

11

CHAMPIONS LEAGUE CURSE

Paris Saint-Germain have clinched the league title on nine occasions. It has almost become an expectation for them to win every year. Because of this the club has set its sights on

not only conquering Ligue 1, but winning the Champions League. With record-breaking transfers such as the purchase of Neymar Jr. and Kylian, the club hoped to transform from the best team in France to a European superpower.

It's hard to argue that PSG are not one of the best teams in Europe. With Kylian on their team anything is possible. Yet getting their hands on the Champions League trophy, despite their talented squad, has proved difficult. In Kylian's first season with the club, during the

2017/2018 campaign, PSG were knocked out of the competition in the round of 16. They had lost to Real Madrid 5-2 on aggregate, with Kylian playing against his childhood idol, Cristiano Ronaldo. Yet in this tie Ronaldo was the villain rather than the hero—with the talented forward scoring three of Real Madrid's goals over the two legs.

Kylian and PSG then fell at the exact same hurdle in the 2018/2019 season. To everyone's surprise PSG were knocked out of the competition by Manchester United. Kylian and

PSG played well in the first leg and returned from Old Trafford with a 0-2 win. Kylian had got his name on the scoresheet following a darting run through the middle to fire the ball into the net. But things did not go to plan in Paris. PSG were defeated on away goals following a 1-3 loss, with Manchester United's Marcus Rashford scoring a late penalty to eliminate Kylian and PSG.

The 2019/2020 Champions League season appeared to be the year that Kylian could break PSG's curse. He led

the team far beyond the round of 16 where they had previously fallen, and all the way to the Champions League final. There, they came up against a stern opponent in Bayern Munich.

Due to the COVID-19 pandemic, there were no fans in attendance to cheer on either side. In the end, the game was settled by a single goal. Bayern Munich's Kingsley Coman scored a header in the second half to break French hearts and continue the Champions League curse.

In the 2020/2021 campaign, Kylian avenged his previous year's demons

by scoring a hat trick against Bayern Munich in the quarterfinal. With last year's winners out of the way, the path seemed clear for Kylian and his team to triumph. However, there was one more twist in PSG's Champions League journey.

PSG faced Manchester City in the semifinals and were defeated 1-2 in the first leg. There was still hope that the team would turn things around in the second leg, but trouble wasn't far away. In between the games, Kylian received a knock during a Ligue 1 fixture and was unable to play

in the Champions League second leg. Without their star forward present, Manchester City picked PSG apart.

Kylian is young and has the talent and years ahead of him to achieve a Champions League triumph. But will he break the curse at PSG or have to move elsewhere to get his hands on the Champions League trophy?

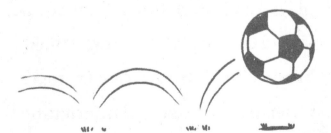

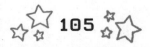

12

EURO 2020

While Kylian didn't taste victory in the Champions League, he certainly did in a previous major international tournament. Having played a massive role in France's 2018 World Cup win, the young striker headed into Euro 2020 with hopes of securing his second international

title. However, France was placed in the so called 'Group of Death'.

In major tournaments, all countries battle it out in a group stage. Each group has four teams all trying to make it to the knockout rounds. In Euro 2020, France were, on paper, in the toughest group of all. To emerge from the group stage, they needed to perform against Portugal, Germany and Hungary.

The first side standing in their way was Germany—a team with years of success on their side. But in recent years Germany had started to

lose their edge and had sometimes crumbled during matches. However, they were still one of the strongest sides in the tournament. It was a team filled with rising talents such as Kai Havertz and Timo Werner.

In the 19th minute of the match, Pogba played a delicate through ball with the outside of his right foot into the left of the penalty box. Lucas Hernández brought the ball under his control and fired it across the box. Kylian sprinted with all his might to reach it, and he was going to get there. Seeing that his team was

in trouble, German defender Mats Hummels stuck out his leg to stop the attack. But with Kylian lurking behind him, all he could do was put the ball into his own net. In the tightly fought contest, France were able to get their tournament off to the perfect start with a 0-1 win.

However, things did not go to plan in France's second match. "Les Bleus" faced off against the supposed weakest team of the group: Hungary. Playing at their home stadium in Budapest, with 67,000 fans cheering them on, Hungary put on one of the

country's best ever performances. They held France, the reigning world champions, to a 1-1 draw.

Next, France was held to yet another draw in their final group stage match. They faced the competition's reigning champions, Portugal, who won Euro 2016. Thanks to a brace from Cristiano Ronaldo, matched by Karim Benzema for France, they drew at 2-2 and both sides shared the points. France finished at the top of their group, and Portugal also made it to the knockout rounds as one of the best third-

place teams. The top two teams from each group, as well as the four best third-place teams, progress to the round of 16.

By finishing first in their group, France were placed in what is often thought of as a preferred position in the round of 16. France were placed against Switzerland—a team far below them in the world rankings, and a team that most people expected them to beat. But the stubborn Swiss side were not going to be knocked out of the competition easily. On the 28th

of June, at the Arena Națională in Bucharest, the two teams played in one of the most memorable matches of the tournament.

In the 15th minute, Switzerland striker, Haris Seferović, leapt higher than any of the French defenders and met a cross with his forehead. He nodded the ball toward goal like an arrow. The net rippled. It was 0-1 as Switzerland took a shock lead!

Going into the second half, the Swiss underdogs were barely troubled at their end of the field. The Swiss wingback Steven Zuber, who

had been a nightmare for the French defenders, went on an incredible run down the touchline. Benjamin Pavard, the French defender, slid in to try and steal the ball. But he completely missed and took out Zuber. The referee didn't notice the incident but was made to check VAR. After rewatching on the screen, with every fan in the stadium holding their breath, he pointed to the spot!

Switzerland had a penalty and a great opportunity to double their lead. Ricardo Rodríguez volunteered to take the penalty. If he scored,

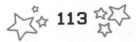

surely France would have too much ground to make up? Surely it would be Switzerland's match?

Rodríguez struck the ball. But instead of hitting the net, it smacked against the outstretched hand of the French goalkeeper! Lloris had saved his team and the score was still 0-1. The French fans in the stadium erupted as if they'd score a goal rather than saved one. France were still in the game

 and had every possibility of turning the match around.

With a newfound confidence, France did exactly that. Only two minutes later, Kylian played the ball to Benzema in the box. Benzema brought the ball under his control with an out-of-this-world touch, and dinked the ball past the onrushing goalkeeper. *Goal!* The teams were level at 1-1.

The drama was far from over. Minutes later Kylian played a neat one-two with Griezmann in the penalty box. Kylian backheeled the ball to Griezmann who ran at goal and tried to chip the goalkeeper.

At the back post was Benzema, who waited for the ball to drop before heading it into the net. *Goal!* In a matter of minutes, France had gone from almost being 0-2 down to leading 2-1. Soccer fans across the world could not believe what they were seeing. When France needed to show their quality, they did it.

In the 75th minute, Pogba shone. The talented midfielder struck a phenomenal curved strike from outside of the box. It fired into the top right corner, leaving the French fans breathless. It was 3-1 with only

fifteen minutes left to play. Surely the match was now France's and they were heading into the quarterfinals? But it was a rollercoaster match, with the fans on the edges of their seats, and the determined Swiss side simply refused to be beaten.

In the 81st minute, Switzerland grabbed a goal back, thanks to another Seferović header. As the game approached ninety minutes, the French fans watched nervously. But the Swiss fans cheered as loudly as they could to spur their team on for one last attack.

Pogba was tackled in the center of the field and the Swiss players broke into the opposition half. With each step, time was running out. Granit Xhaka played a defense-splitting pass through the middle of the field, which was brought under control by Mario Gavranović. The substitute sent the French defender Presnel Kimpembe to the ground with a neat touch and fired the ball at the goal. Lloris could not meet the ball, even at a full stretch. It struck the net. *Goal!* The Swiss players ran across the field with joy greater than any

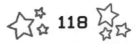

they'd experienced in their soccer careers. They'd brought themselves back level, and this match was not finished yet.

The whistle blew for full time and extra time had to be played. But neither side scored in the additional thirty minutes. This tie had to be settled by penalties. The first nine penalty takers all struck the back of the net with their efforts. Switzerland scored all five, and France all four of their penalties.

Kylian—a hero for France in 2018— was France's fifth penalty taker.

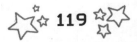

He took the ball from his supportive
goalkeeper and placed it down
on the spot. As he did so, it was
clear that his hands were shaking.
The young star stood before the
goal with the hopes of an entire
country on his shoulders. He tried
to shut out the noise and shouts in
the stadium. Kylian ran up to the
ball and placed it to the left. But
instead of the net, the ball met the
Swiss goalkeeper's gloves with a
thunderous thud. Kylian stood with
the whole world watching. His heart
sank.

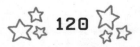

Switzerland shocked the world by knocking France—and Kylian Mbappé—out of the tournament. As the Swiss players and fans celebrated one of the best nights of their lives, Kylian stood in disbelief, wanting to be anywhere but in that stadium.

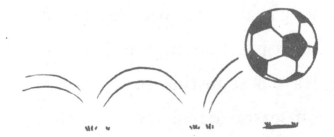

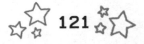

13

ROAD TO QATAR 2022

With the European Championships long over, Kylian was beginning to move past that night in Bucharest. He took some time for himself in the off-season to recharge his batteries.

One night, as the city of Paris was starting to sleep, Kylian slipped out of his house. He went to a private indoor leisure center to play sports. But he wasn't alone. He was joined by his younger brother, Ethan.

Kylian wasn't the only member of the family on PSG's books. Ethan Mbappé played for PSG's academy.

"So I've heard good things coming out of the academy," said Kylian.

"Like what?" asked Ethan.

"That you're at least 10% as good as I am," he said.

Ethan threw a ball at

Kylian and he ducked. The pair of them laughed as it bounced across the court.

"Ten times better more like," said Ethan.

But it wasn't soccer that the pair were playing. Basketball held a special place in Kylian's heart. Before the COVID-19 pandemic, Kylian liked to visit the United States and watch basketball games whenever he could. He would attend them wearing the latest in sporting fashion. Being one of the most recognizable faces in world

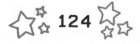

soccer meant that all sports brands and fashion designers wanted Kylian to wear their clothing. And as someone who had an obsession with the latest trainers, it was certainly a perk of the job for Kylian. He had so many pairs of shoes he'd lost count!

Kylian's latest trainers squeaked on the court as he dribbled the ball past his brother and took a shot. The ball bounced off the backboard and rippled through the net.

"Do you think you'll ever leave Paris?" asked Ethan.

"I love it here," said Kylian. "But I guess you can never rule it out. Why?"

"No reason," said Ethan. "It'll just be funny when you get benched for me if I make the first team."

Kylian pushed his younger brother and laughed.

"I like the confidence," said Kylian.

"Let's play again. I'm winning this time," said Ethan.

"We'll see about that," Kylian grinned.

On the court, with his brother, Kylian felt like a child again. Having been thrown into the spotlight at

such a young age, he'd had to grow up quickly to succeed in the tough world of professional soccer.

★ ★ ★

Kylian has achieved so much at such a young age, and he has so many years of soccer left. He grew up idolizing Cristiano Ronaldo and has now faced him on multiple occasions. Will Kylian be able to match the achievements of his idol? Will the young man from Bondy break even his records?